6.3/0.5

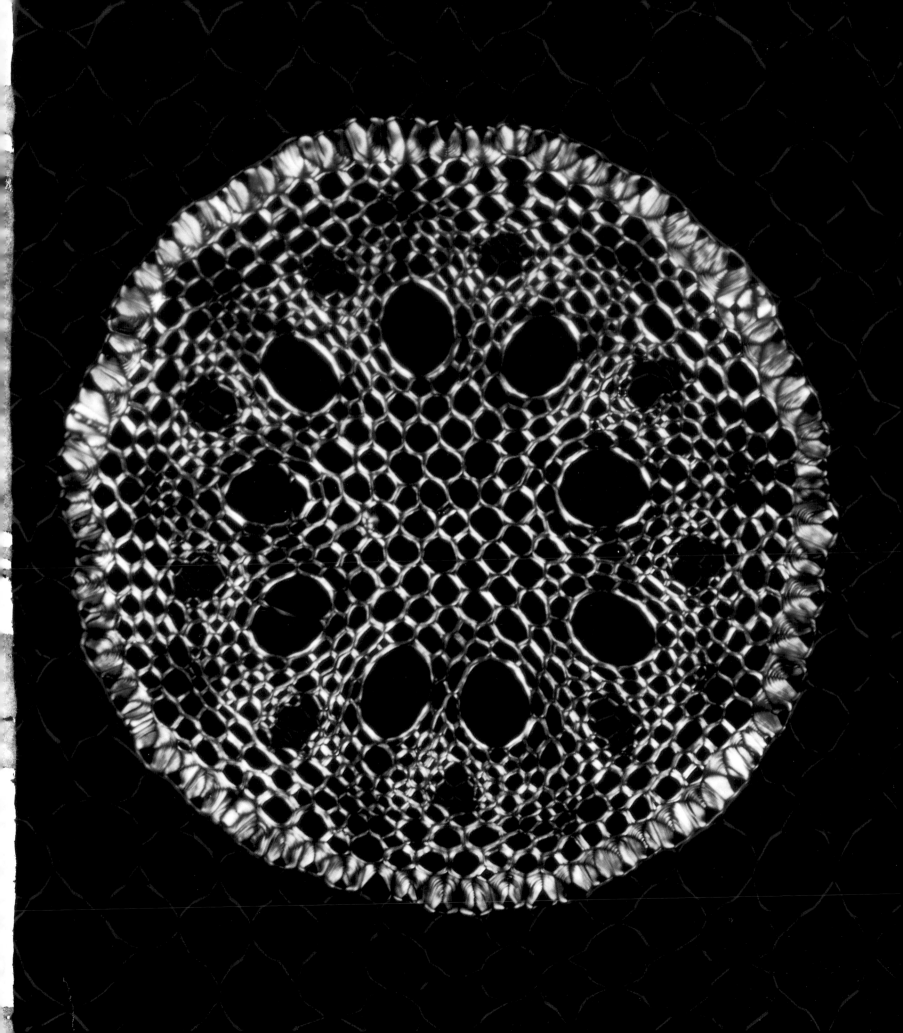

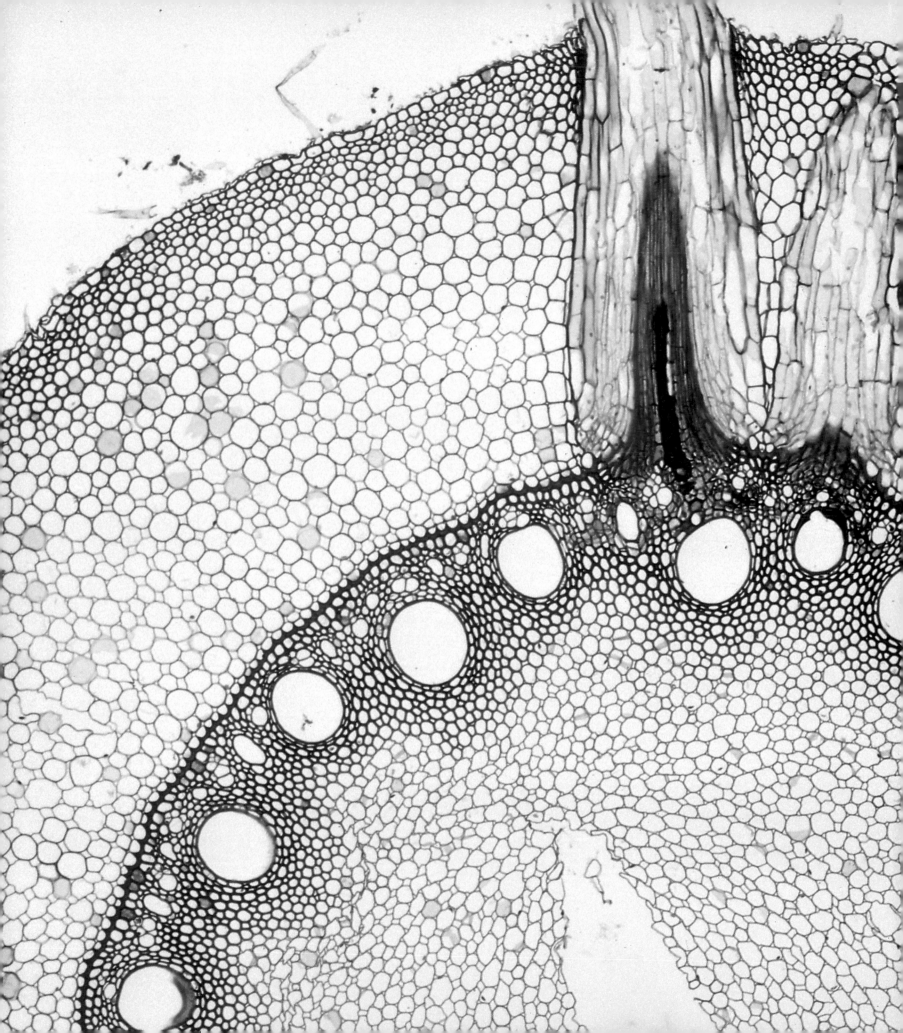

CREATIVE EDUCATION

Cells

Michael George

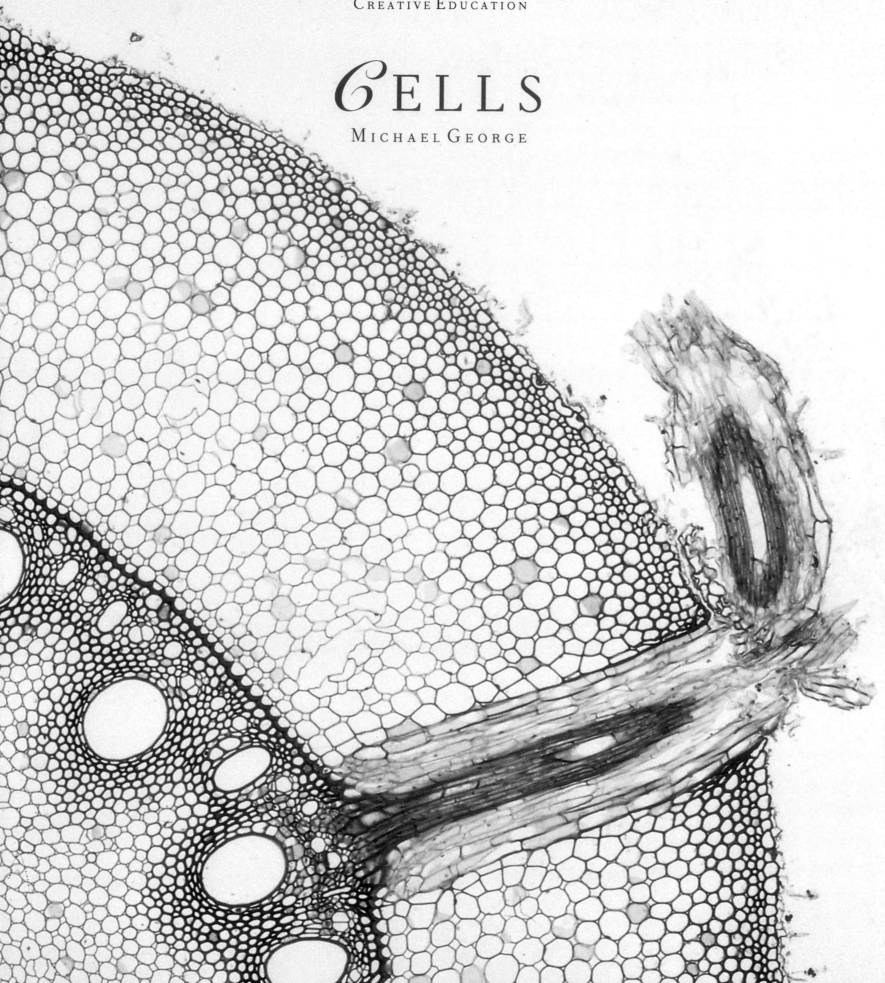

Designed by Rita Marshall
with the help of Thomas Lawton
© 1992 Creative Education, Inc.
123 South Broad Street,
Mankato, Minnesota 56001

Photography by Peter Arnold,
Comstock, Dwight Kuhn, Photo
Researchers, Tom Stack, and
Visuals Unlimited.

Library of Congress
Cataloging-in-Publication Data

George, Michael, 1964–
Cells / by Michael George.
*   p.   cm.*
Summary: Describes the parts of a
cell, their functions, and the different
kinds of cells.
ISBN 0-88682-437-0
1. Cells—Juvenile literature.
[1. Cells.] I. Title.   91-11774
QH582.5.G46   1991   CIP
574.87—dc20   AC

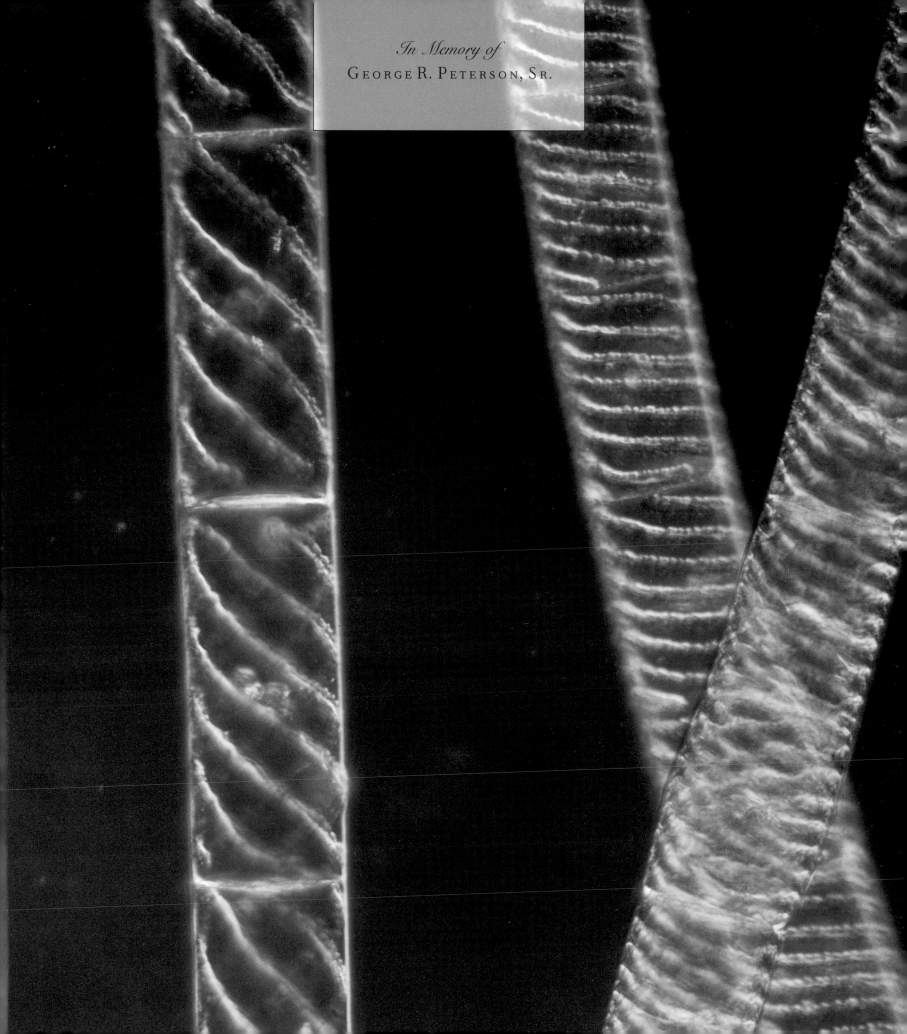

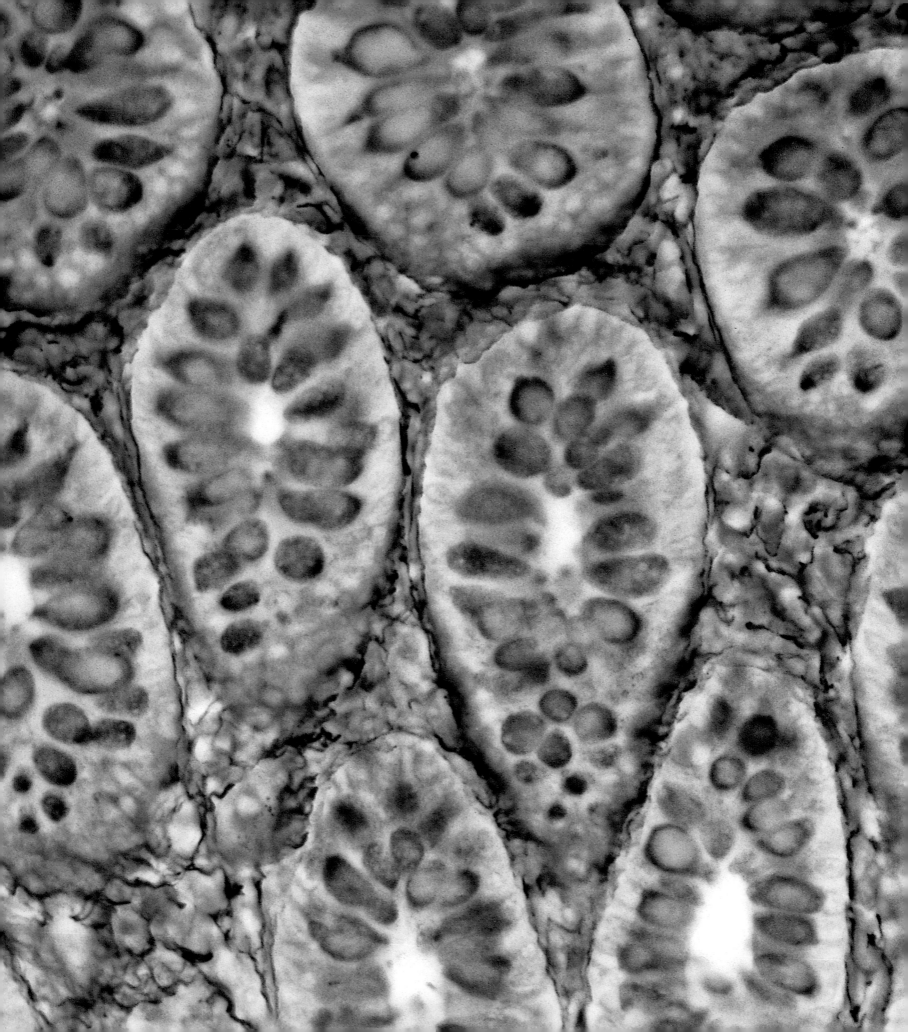

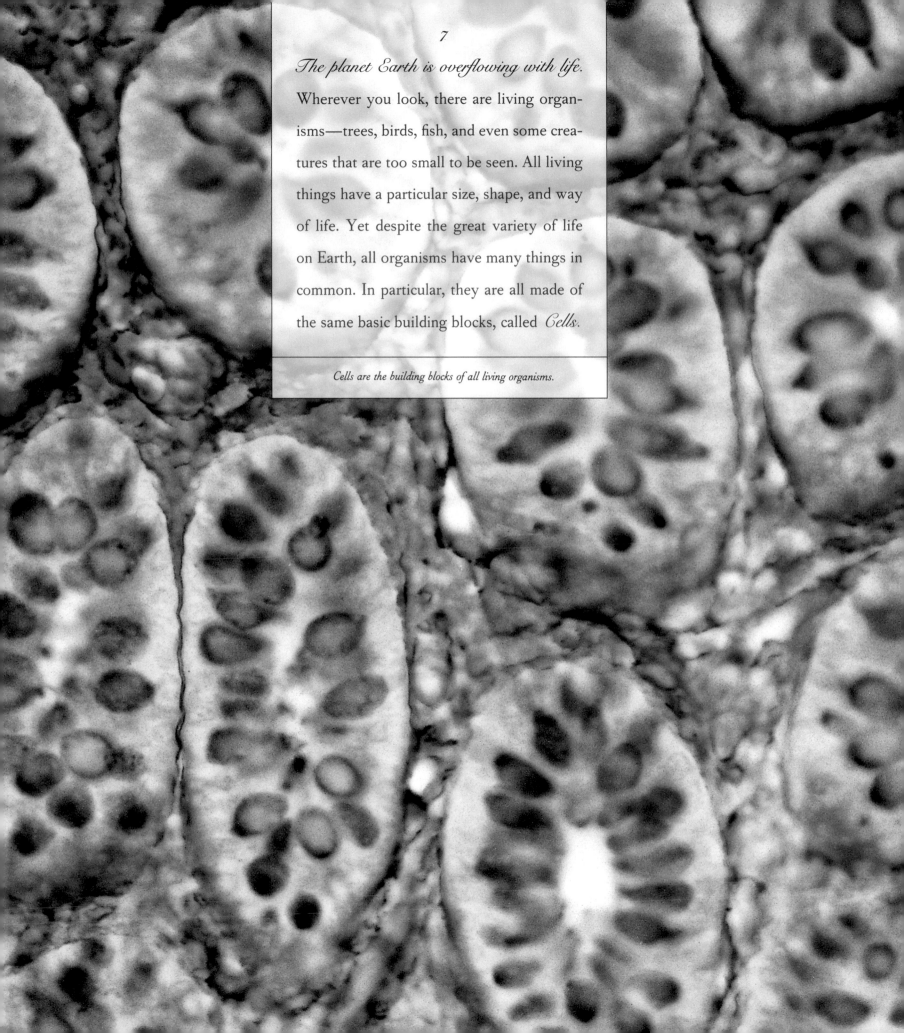

The planet Earth is overflowing with life. Wherever you look, there are living organisms—trees, birds, fish, and even some creatures that are too small to be seen. All living things have a particular size, shape, and way of life. Yet despite the great variety of life on Earth, all organisms have many things in common. In particular, they are all made of the same basic building blocks, called *Cells.*

Cells are the building blocks of all living organisms.

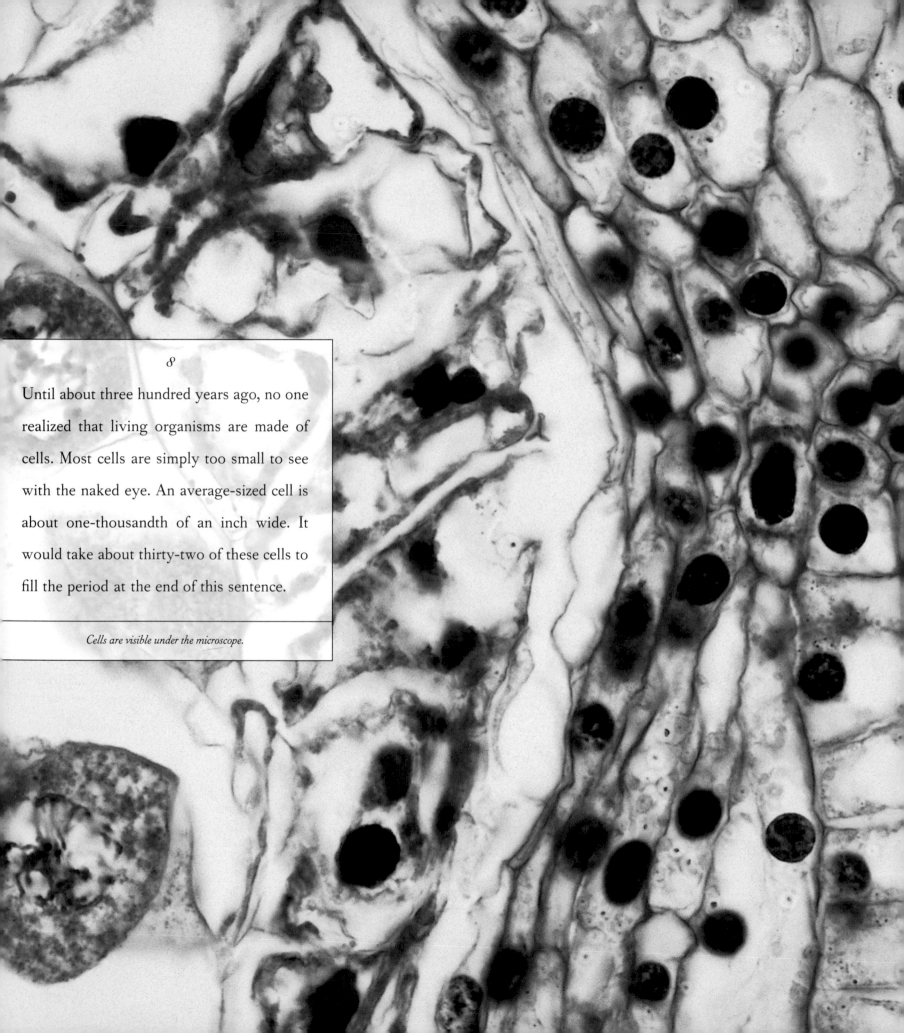

Until about three hundred years ago, no one realized that living organisms are made of cells. Most cells are simply too small to see with the naked eye. An average-sized cell is about one-thousandth of an inch wide. It would take about thirty-two of these cells to fill the period at the end of this sentence.

Cells are visible under the microscope.

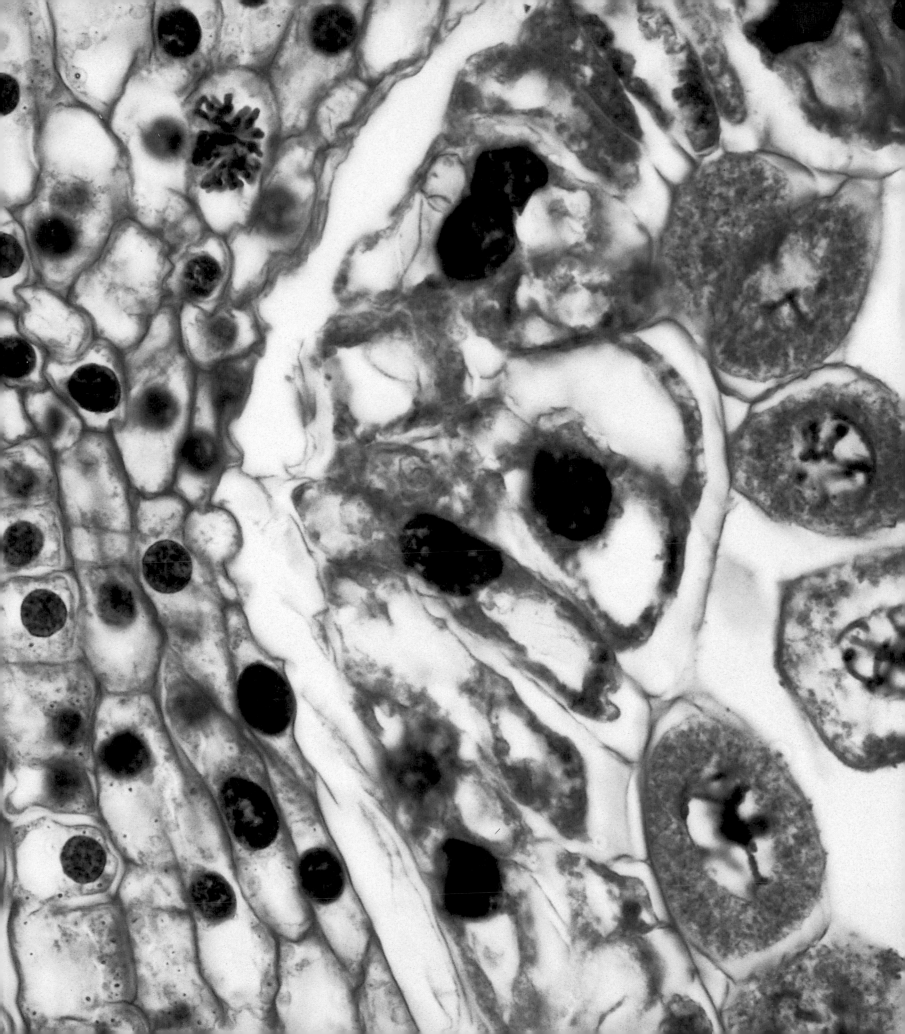

In the late 1600s, Anton van Leeuwenhoek constructed the world's first high-powered *Microscope*. It magnified the images of objects nearly three hundred times their normal size. Using his microscope, Leeuwenhoek peered into the world of little things. He made some startling discoveries. When he placed a drop of rainwater under the microscope, he saw tiny creatures swimming about. When he looked at a drop of blood, he saw countless saucer-shaped blobs. And when he examined a piece of skin, he saw something that resembled the bricks in a cobblestone road. Without knowing it, Leeuwenhoek was the first person to see cells.

Page 10: Hair under a microscope.
Page 11: The magnified surface of a fingertip.

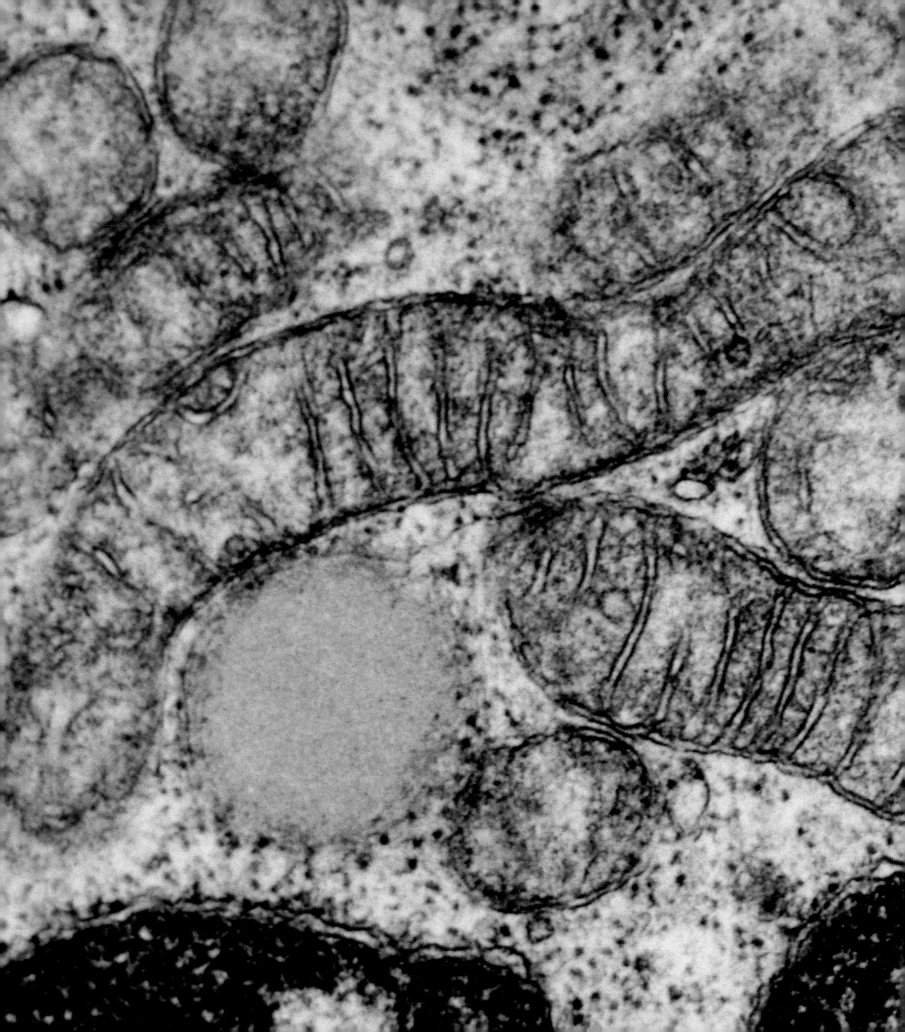

Since the time of Leeuwenhoek, scientists have determined that all living things are made of cells. The simplest organisms consist of a single, solitary cell. These tiny creatures, called *Microbes,* can be found in the air, in a drop of pond water, and at the bottom of the ocean. They live in frozen glaciers and in scorching deserts. Some one-celled organisms even live in your hair, on your skin, and inside your body.

Amazingly, a one-celled organism can do many of the things that a human body can do. It can make or catch food, eliminate wastes, grow, and react to changes in the environment. A one-celled organism can even reproduce. By dividing, the single cell becomes two.

Inside a single cell.

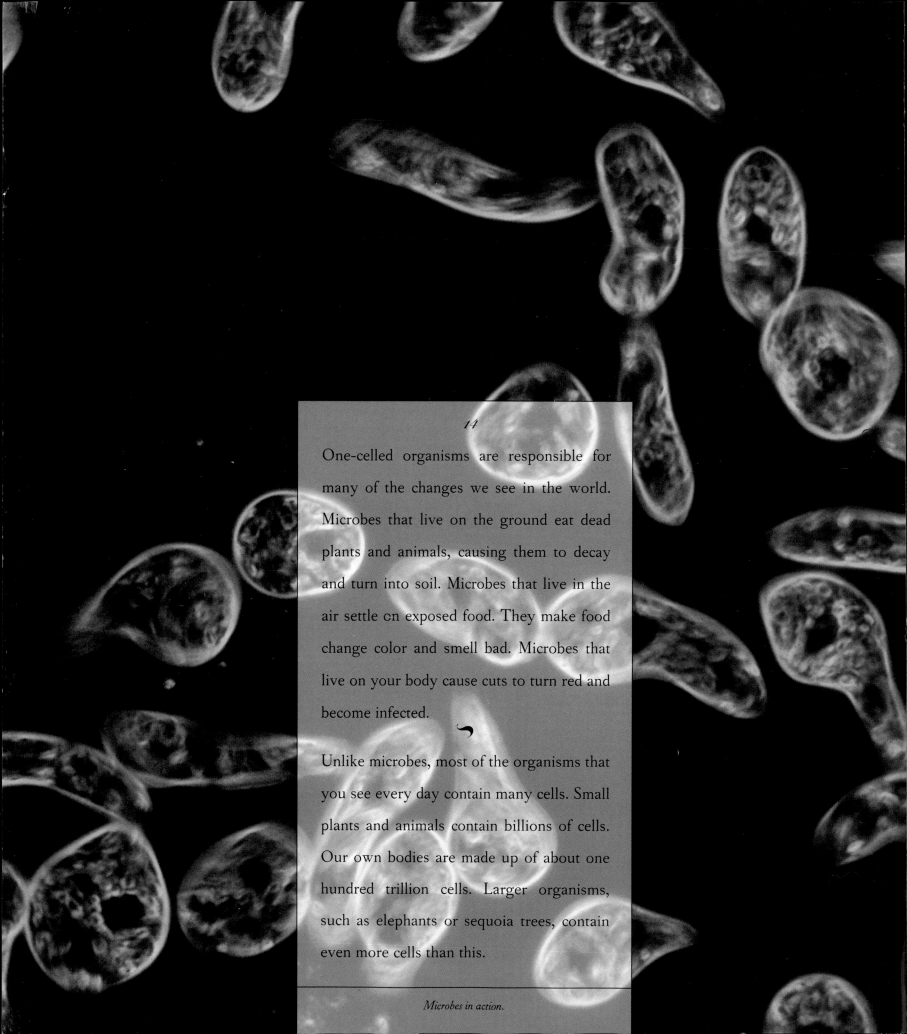

One-celled organisms are responsible for many of the changes we see in the world. Microbes that live on the ground eat dead plants and animals, causing them to decay and turn into soil. Microbes that live in the air settle on exposed food. They make food change color and smell bad. Microbes that live on your body cause cuts to turn red and become infected.

Unlike microbes, most of the organisms that you see every day contain many cells. Small plants and animals contain billions of cells. Our own bodies are made up of about one hundred trillion cells. Larger organisms, such as elephants or sequoia trees, contain even more cells than this.

Microbes in action.

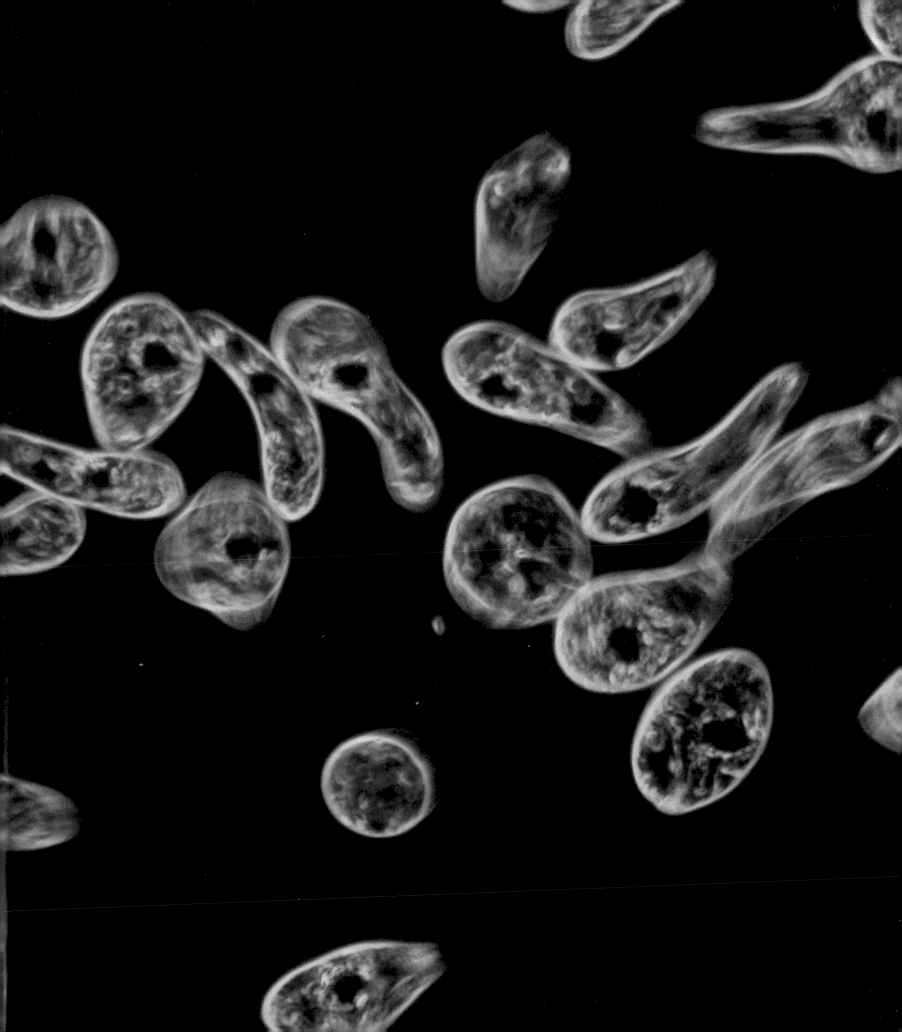

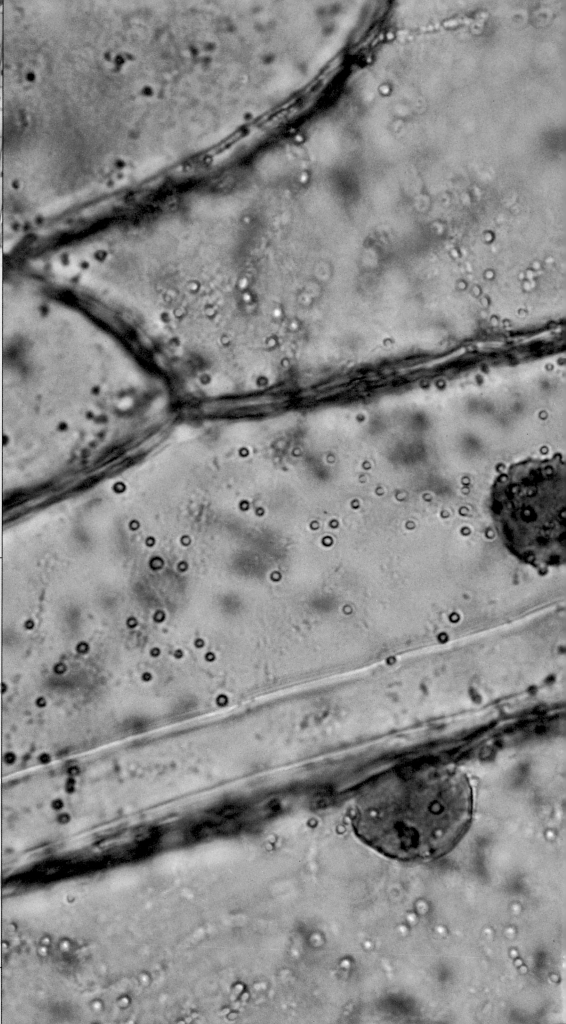

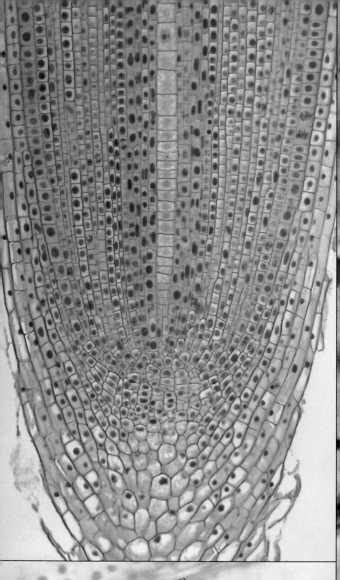

Plants and animals contain many different kinds of cells, each type performing a specific job. Some of the cells in many-celled organisms are designed for protection. One type of protective cell is *Leaf Epidermis,* found on the outside of leaves. Leaf epidermis cells fit together like the pieces of a jigsaw puzzle. They are covered with a waxy, waterproof coating that prevents leaves from drying out. Leaf epidermis cells also protect leaves from dangerous germs and injury.

The epidermis cells of an onion.
Inset: Onion root cells.

People also have epidermis cells, better known as skin cells. Skin cells are thin and flat. They are stacked upon each other like pancakes. It takes billions of skin cells to cover your whole body. You have more than ten million skin cells on your hand alone. Like leaf epidermis cells, skin cells prevent our bodies from drying out and protect us from germs and injury.

19

When you have a cut or a scratch, germs can get past your body's skin cells. If this happens, another type of cell comes to the rescue. These cells, called *Leukocytes,* look like formless blobs of jelly. They can actually change shape, enabling them to surround and engulf dangerous germs. Leukocytes die after destroying many germs. They collect near infections and become visible, as pus.

The skin cells of a pig.

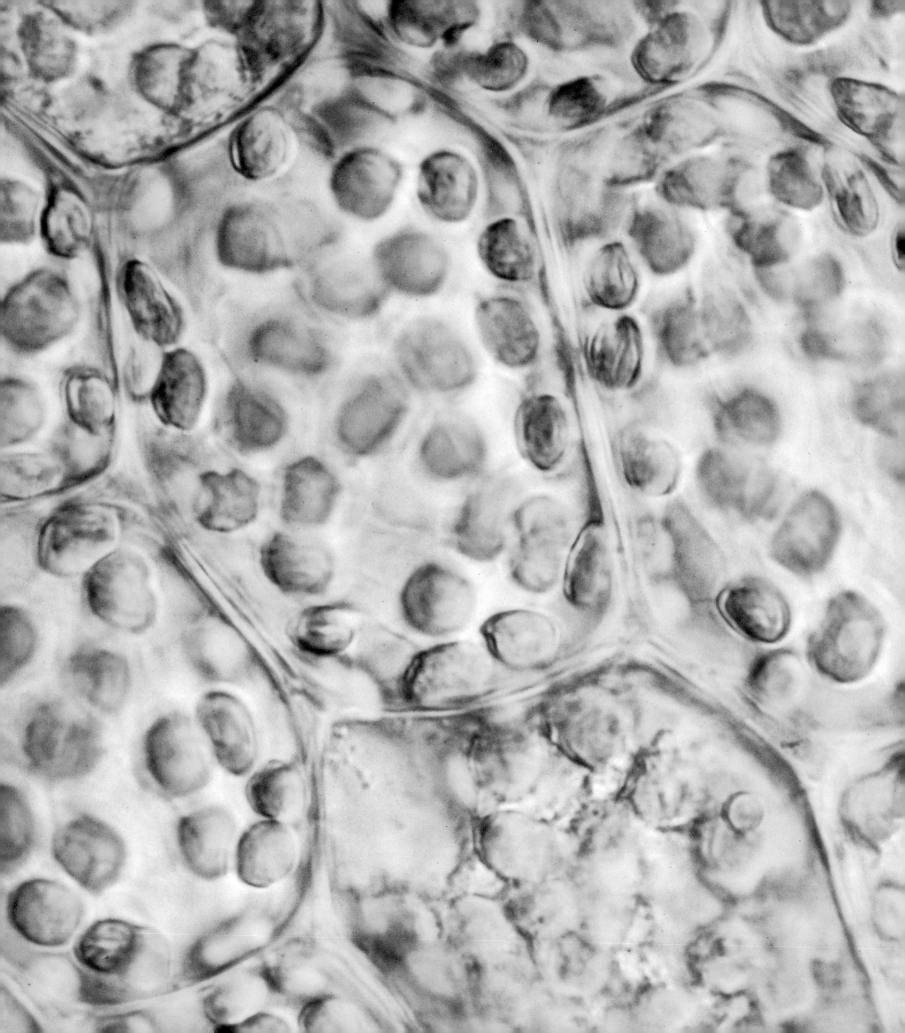

In order for plants and animals to grow to any stature, they need some method of support. All plant cells have a built-in method of support: they are surrounded by a rigid covering called a *Cell Wall*. The cell wall makes plant cells stiff and strong. Trees and other woody plants have special cells with extra-thick cell walls. These cells give trees additional support, enabling them to grow high above the ground.

Unlike plant cells, animal cells are not reinforced by cell walls. Most animal cells are soft and flexible. As a result, animals need special cells to support their bodies. The framework of your body, your skeleton, is made up of *Bone Cells*. Bone cells are surrounded by a hard material that makes bone stiff and strong. *Cartilage Cells*, which form the gristle on the end of a chicken bone, also provide animals with support.

The yellow walls of moss plant cells.

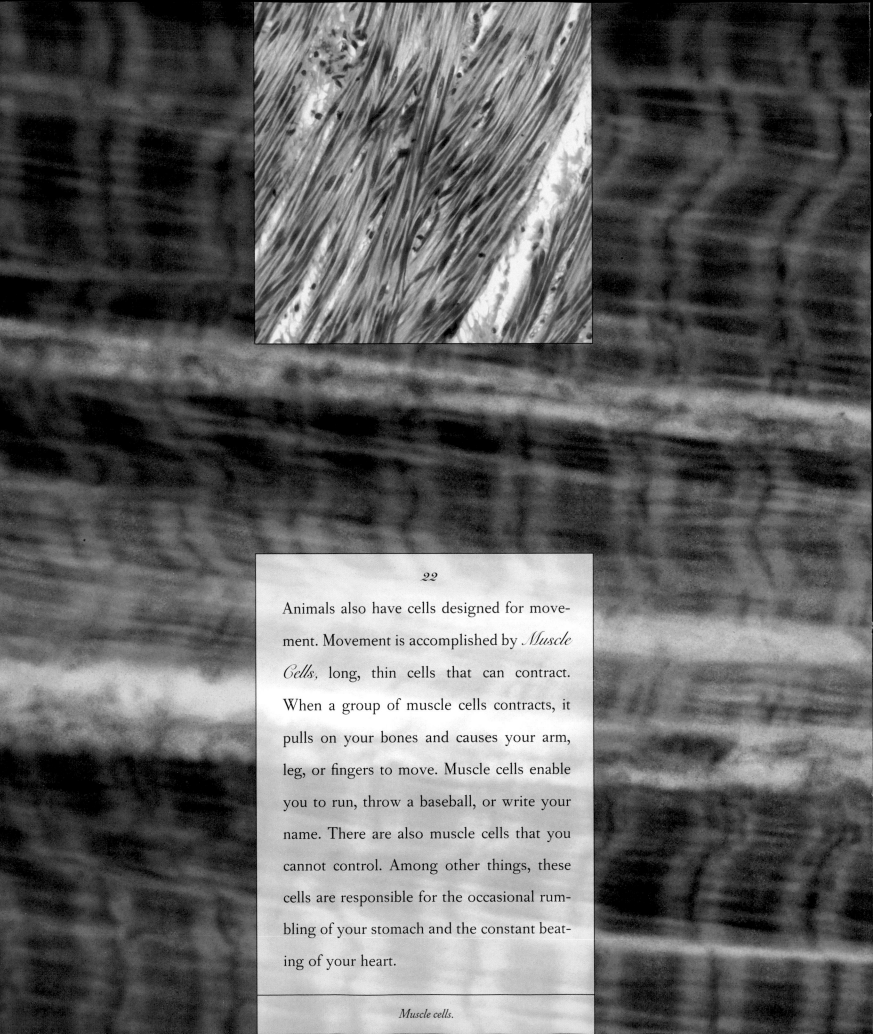

Animals also have cells designed for movement. Movement is accomplished by *Muscle Cells,* long, thin cells that can contract. When a group of muscle cells contracts, it pulls on your bones and causes your arm, leg, or fingers to move. Muscle cells enable you to run, throw a baseball, or write your name. There are also muscle cells that you cannot control. Among other things, these cells are responsible for the occasional rumbling of your stomach and the constant beating of your heart.

Muscle cells.

Like one-celled organisms, the cells in your body need food to survive. In many-celled organisms, individual cells cannot go out and find their own food. Instead, nutrients must be transported to each cell. In most animals, food is dissolved in the bloodstream and is transported to each and every cell. The cells absorb the food and use it to fuel their activities.

In order to function, animal cells also need a constant supply of oxygen. Oxygen is carried through your bloodstream by special cells called *Red Blood Cells*. Red blood cells are shaped like smooth saucers, enabling them to flow through thin veins and arteries without getting stuck. Your body contains an enormous number of red blood cells—a single drop of blood contains more than five million.

Red blood cells, dyed for easier viewing.

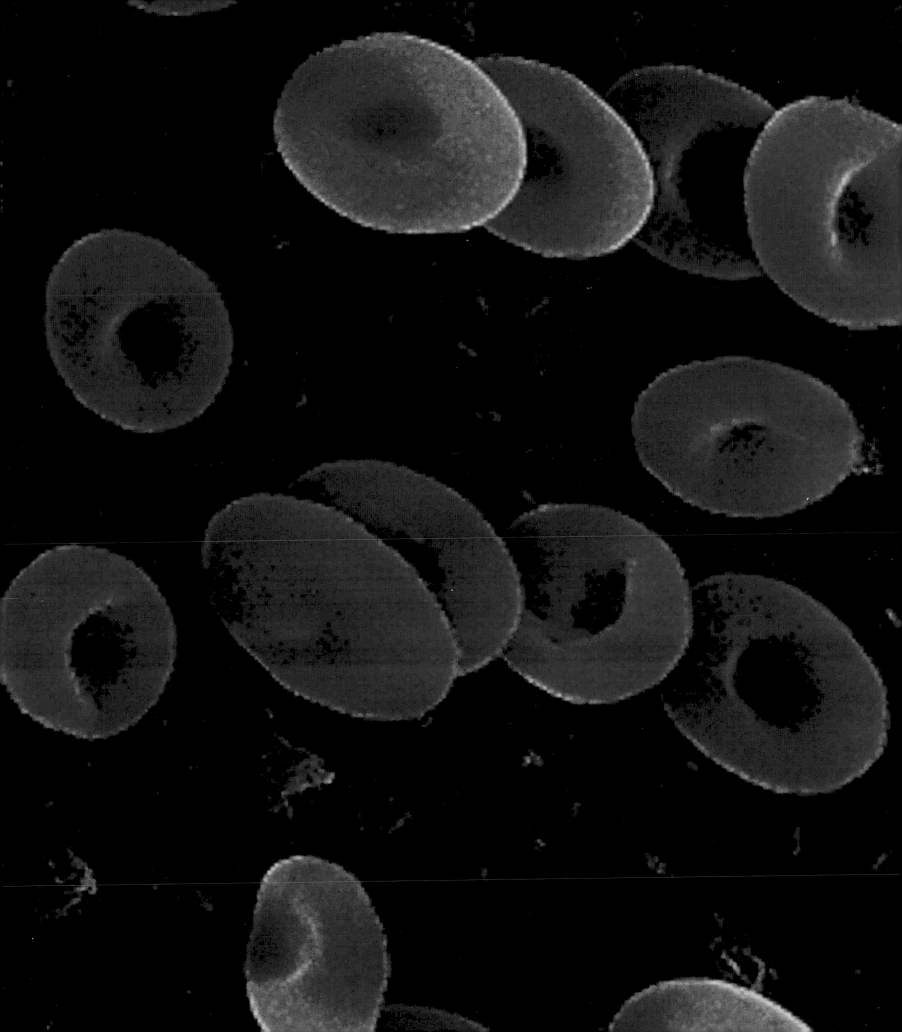

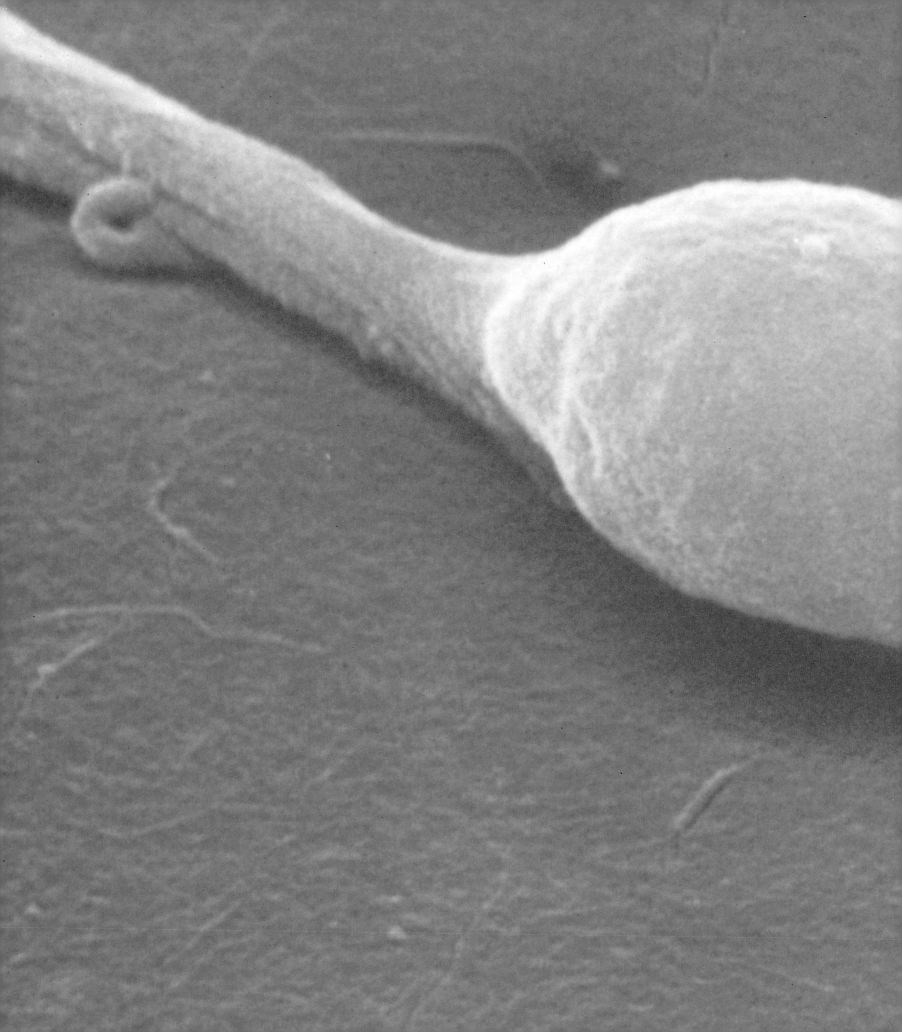

As we have learned, Anton van Leeuwenhoek was the first person to see a cell. He used microscopes that magnified objects about three hundred times their normal size. With them, he could see microbes and skin cells, bone cells and blood cells. However, the microscopes that Leeuwenhoek used were nothing like the ones that scientists use today. In modern laboratories, scientists use microscopes that magnify objects more than one million times. With today's microscopes, scientists can see inside cells.

Human nerve cell.

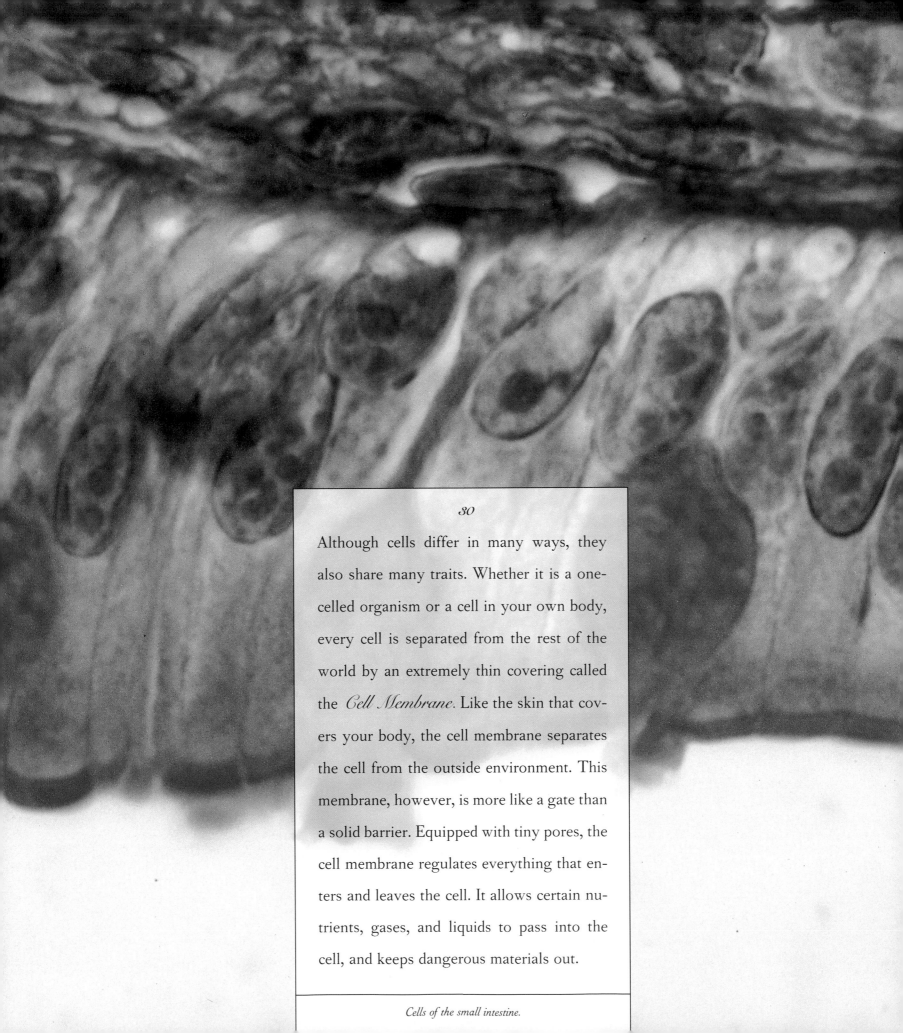

Although cells differ in many ways, they also share many traits. Whether it is a one-celled organism or a cell in your own body, every cell is separated from the rest of the world by an extremely thin covering called the *Cell Membrane*. Like the skin that covers your body, the cell membrane separates the cell from the outside environment. This membrane, however, is more like a gate than a solid barrier. Equipped with tiny pores, the cell membrane regulates everything that enters and leaves the cell. It allows certain nutrients, gases, and liquids to pass into the cell, and keeps dangerous materials out.

Cells of the small intestine.

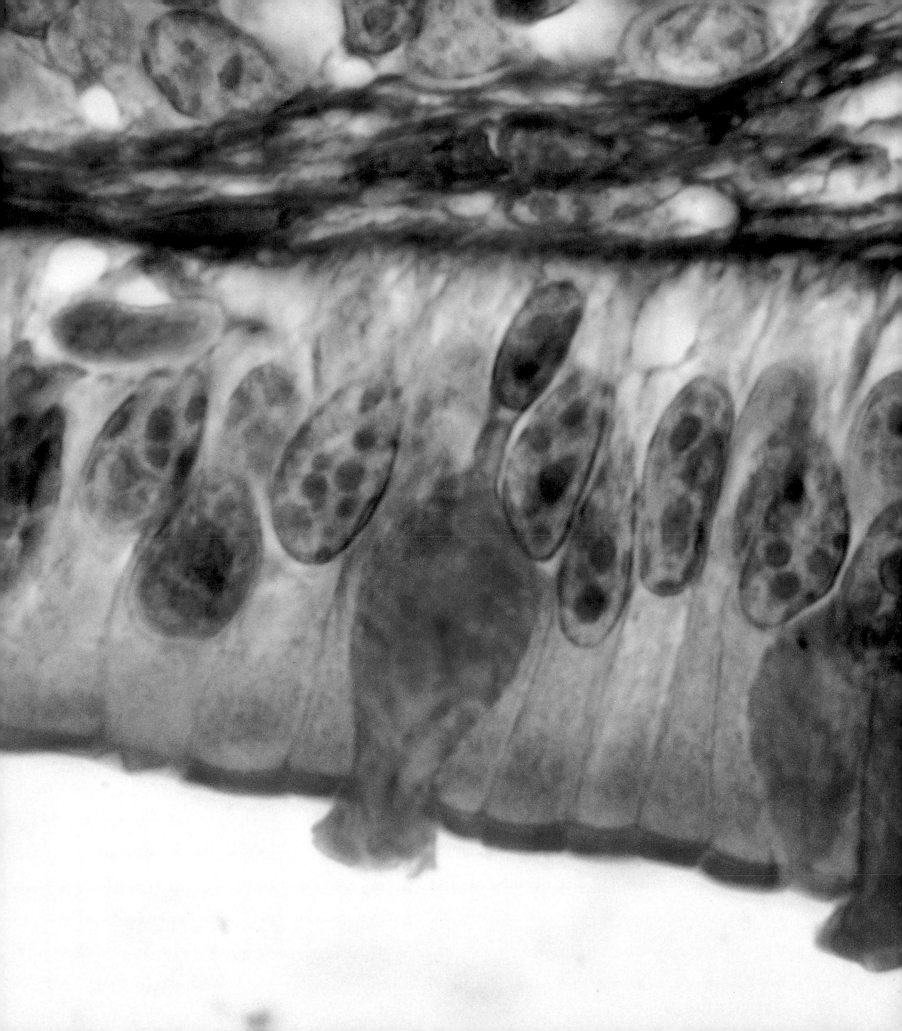

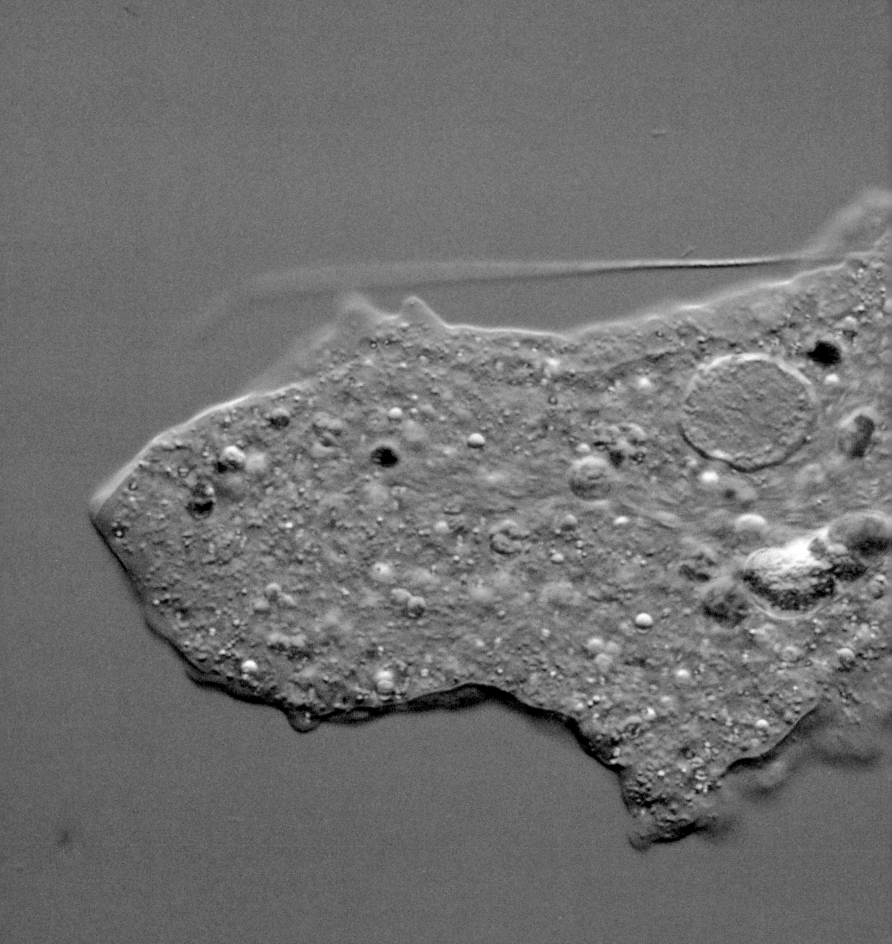

Inside the cell membrane is a grayish, jelly-like substance called *Cytoplasm*. The cytoplasm in most cells consists largely of water, but also contains small amounts of salt, vitamins, and minerals. Also floating throughout the cytoplasm of many cells are tiny structures called *organelles,* meaning "little organs." Like the organs of the human body, each organelle performs a specific activity. One type of organelle digests food. Another packages and transports nutrients. There are also organelles that supply energy for the cell's activities and ones that destroy dangerous germs.

An amoeba moves by changing its body shape.

The biggest, most obvious structure in most cells is called the *Nucleus.* The nucleus is the cell's control center. It contains all the information about what the cell is and what it will be. The nucleus controls the various organelles and issues instructions for most of the cell's activities.

Within each cell, the most basic processes of life take place. Cells digest food, eliminate wastes, produce energy, and respond to changes in their surroundings. They also re-produce. A one-celled organism periodically divides, so that there are two cells where once there was only one. But where do the trillions of cells that form a tree, a fish, or a person come from?

Stomach cells.

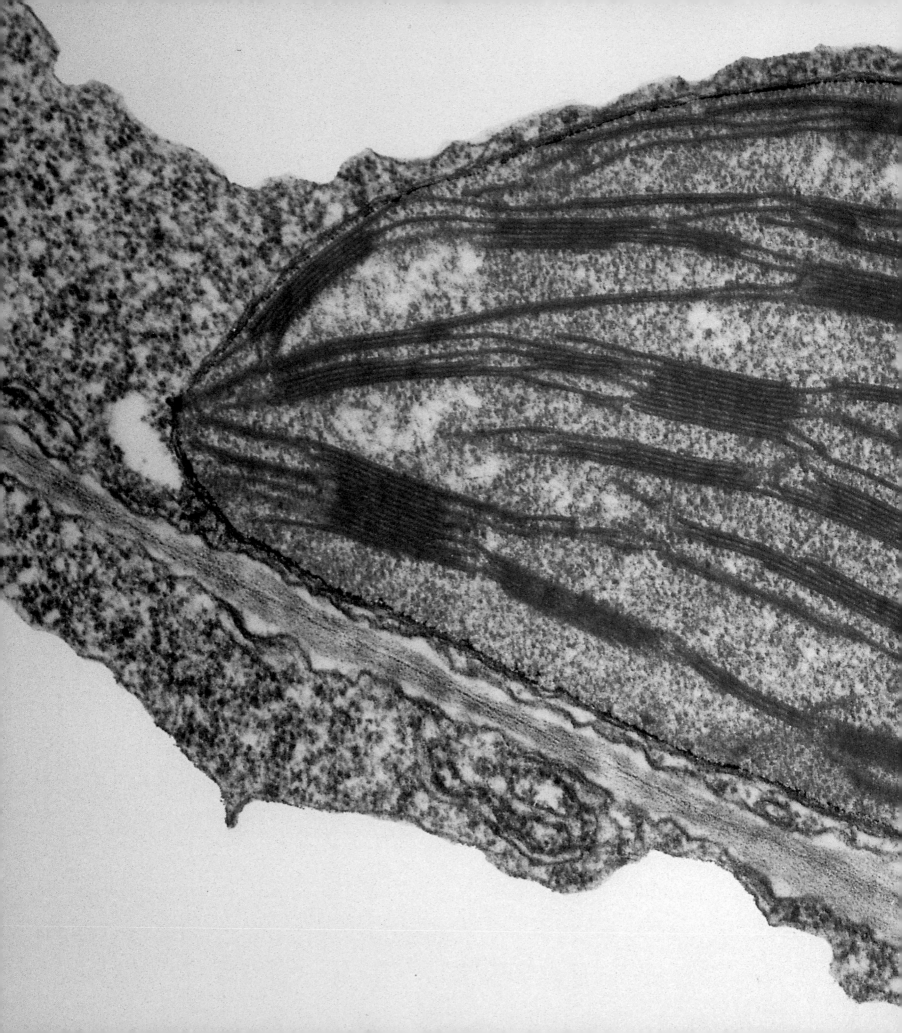

Amazingly, all many-celled organisms begin life as a single cell. The cell from which you originated contained all the instructions on how you were to be made. It contained the information for how many fingers you should have, where your legs should be, and everything else that makes you a human being.

Following these instructions, the cell from which you originated divided, similar to the way a one-celled organism reproduces. Rather than separating, however, the resulting two cells remained attached to each other. After a short time, the two cells divided again, forming four cells. Time after time, the increasing number of cells continued to divide.

Cells of a tobacco leaf.

At some point in your development, your cells began to differentiate. Some became skin cells, some muscle cells, some nerve cells, and so on. Eventually, the different types of cells grouped together. Skin cells combined into skin, muscle cells into muscles, and nerve cells into nerves. Together, all the different cells formed you.

Throughout your entire life, cells in your body continue to divide and form new cells. Every minute, your body produces more than three billion new cells. During the same minute, however, nearly three billion cells wear out and die. Dead skin cells constantly flake off your body, and other worn-out cells pass out with waste products. Most of the new cells that your body produces are made to replace these worn-out cells; the others account for your body's growth.

Nerve cells form the nervous system.

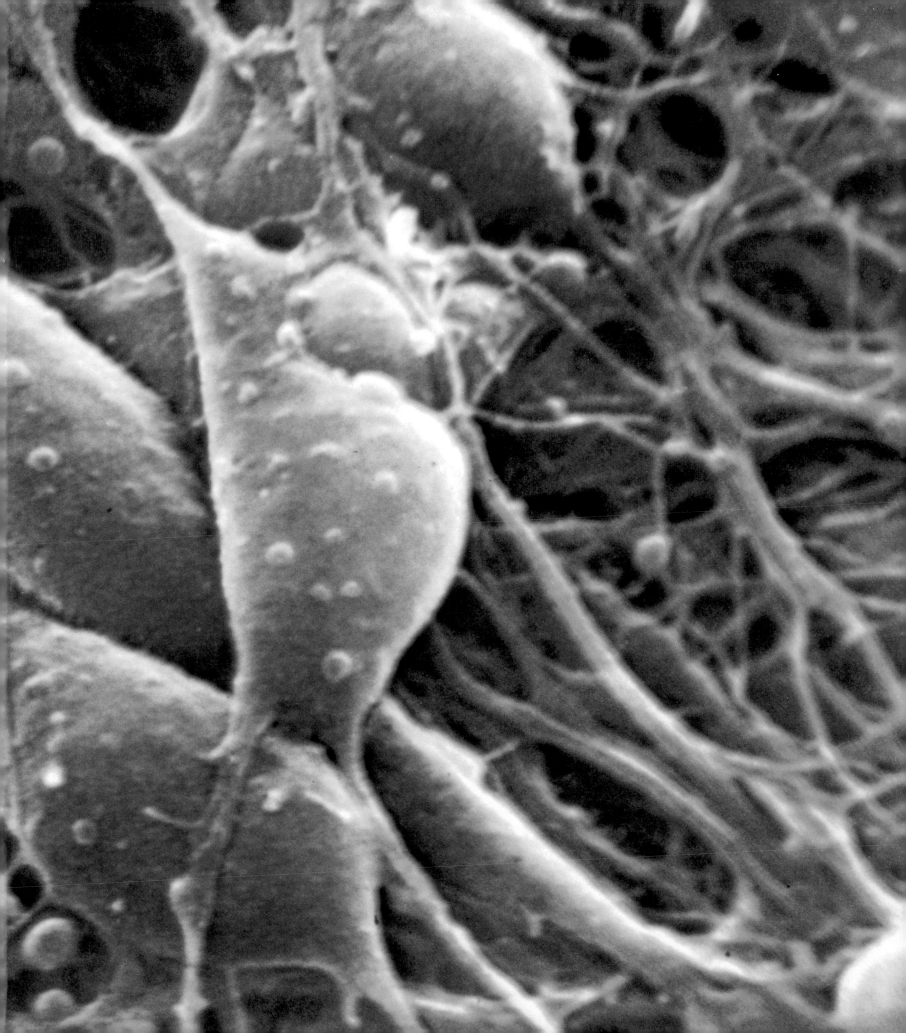

As we have learned, living organisms are made up of one or more cells. *Cells* differ in size, in shape, and in the tasks they perform. However, they also have many things in common. Each cell regulates its own activities and reacts to changes in its environment. Each cell is born and each cell also dies. Thus, a cell is not a lifeless, jellylike blob. Whether it is in your body, in a tree, or is a tiny microbe, the cell in each case is the most basic unit of life.

Neurons relay messages between the brain and the body.